THIS CANDLEWICK BOOK BELONGS TO:

_____

_____

_____

_____

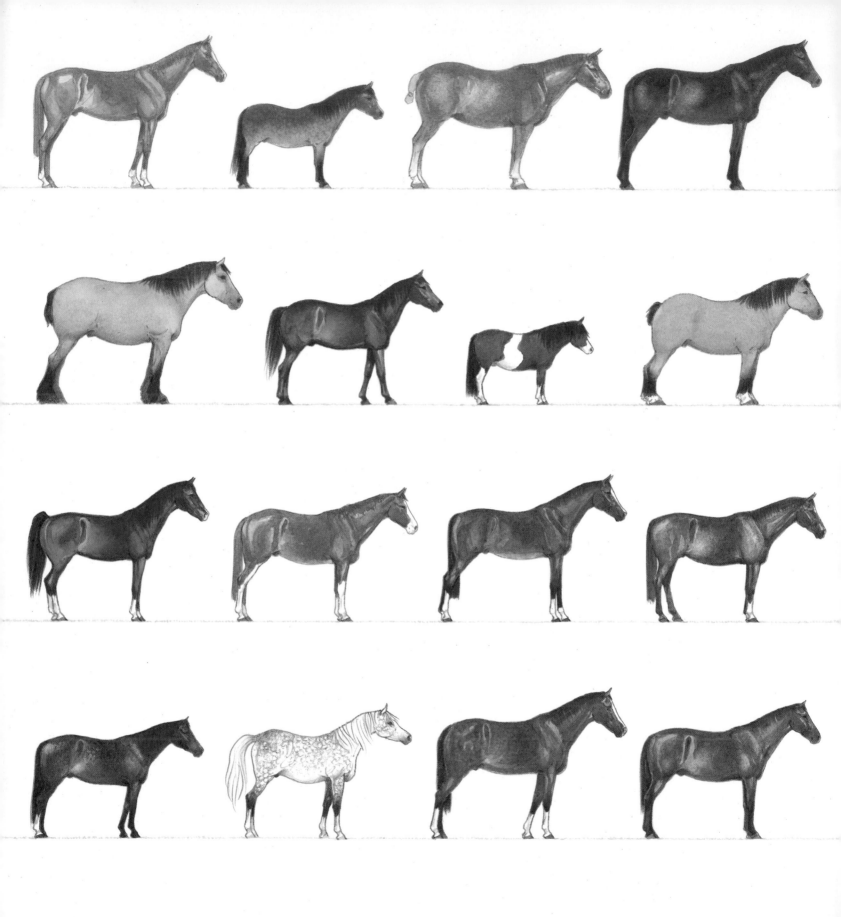

To Cary and April
P.H.
To Kitty
K.L.

Text copyright © 1993 by Peter Hansard
Illustrations copyright © 1993 by Kenneth Lilly

First U.S. paperback edition 1995

Library of Congress Cataloging-in-Publication Data
Hansard, Peter.
A field full of horses / Peter Hansard ; illustrated by Kenneth Lilly.—1st U.S. ed.
(Read and wonder)
Summary: Text and illustrations describe horse behavior, biology, and care.
ISBN 1-56402-302-8 (hardcover)—ISBN 1-56402-527-6 (paperback)
1. Horses—Juvenile literature.   2. Horses—Behavior—Juvenile literature.   [1. Horses.]
I. Lilly, Kenneth, ill. II. Title. III. Series.
SF302.H35   1994   92-45830
636. 1—dc20

2 4 6 8 10 9 7 5 3 1

Printed in Hong Kong

The pictures in this book were done in pencil and watercolor.

Candlewick Press
2067 Massachusetts Avenue
Cambridge, Massachusetts 02140

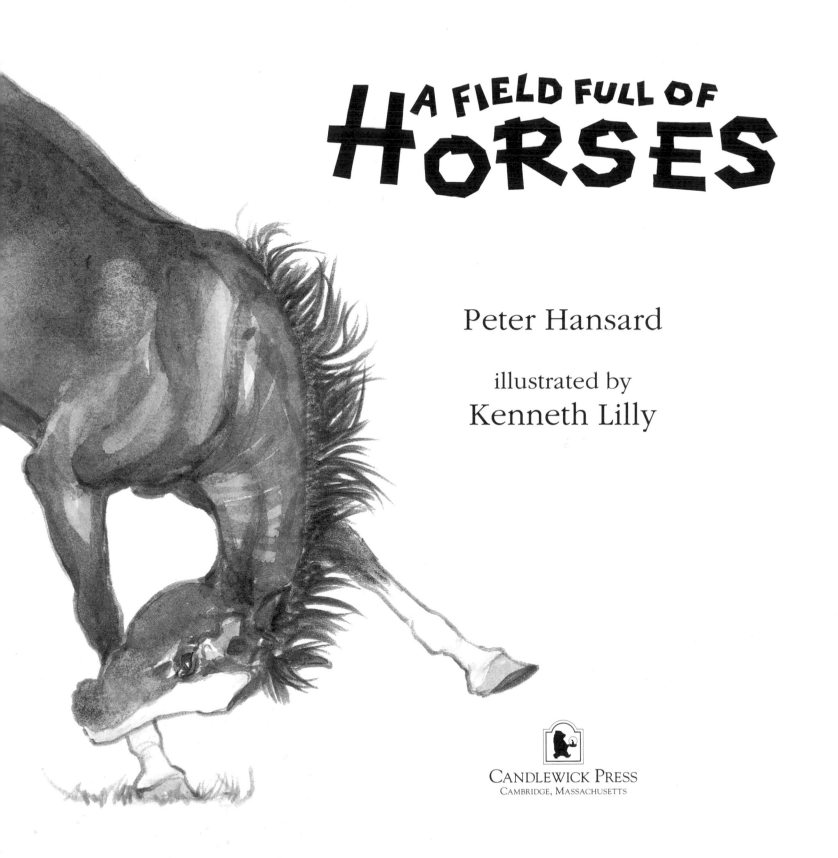

A FIELD FULL OF HORSES

Peter Hansard

illustrated by
Kenneth Lilly

CANDLEWICK PRESS
CAMBRIDGE, MASSACHUSETTS

I walk along the winding lane,
past the tangled willows.
I climb up on the five-barred gate and . . .

there they are.
There's nothing I'd rather do
than just sit and look at horses.

One stands and stamps
in a timothy patch.

One crops the grass with
a champing sound.

In summer,
horses that live outside eat a lot of grass.
In winter, they're given rolled oats,
barley, bran, and hay.

One rolls on her back
in a dusty wallow.

Horses roll in
the dust to help
keep their
coats healthy.

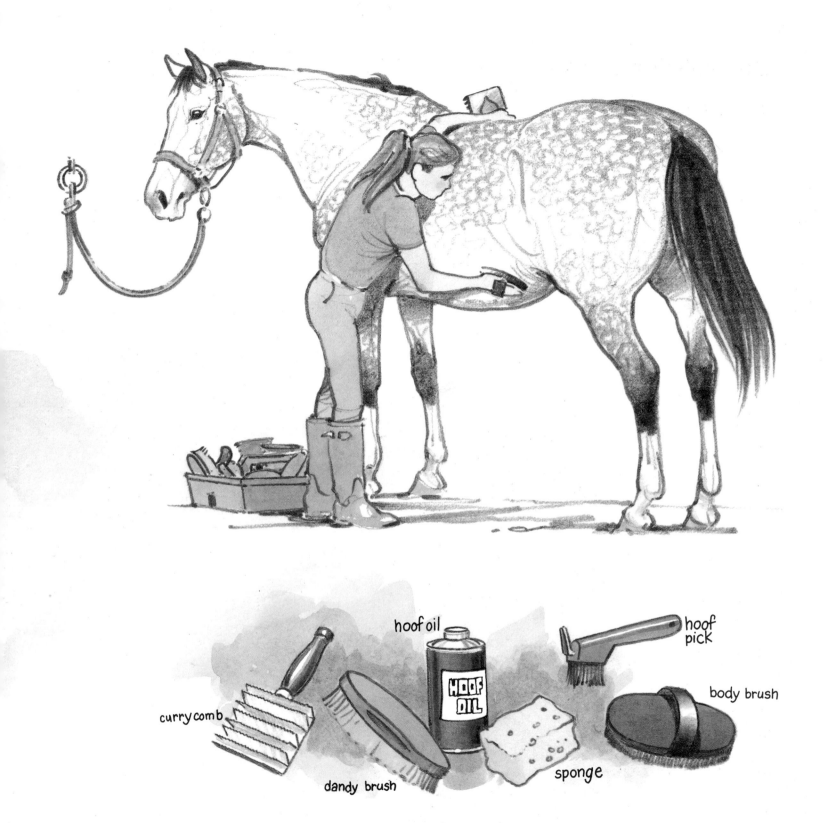

curry comb

hoof oil

hoof pick

dandy brush

HOOF OIL

sponge

body brush

Back at the stables, their owners groom them with tools like these.

One dreams in the shade of a big copper beech
with eyes half shut and tail slowly swishing.

Have you noticed that horses like to rest
with one hind foot up on a turned-back hoof?

One trots up to see if I have apples in my pockets.
She's my favorite and I wish that she were mine.

A grown-up female horse
is called a mare.

A grown-up male horse
is called a stallion.

Her eyes are big and soft, her nostrils flared
and sniffing, and every now and then
she gives a sudden shiver
to keep the flies away.

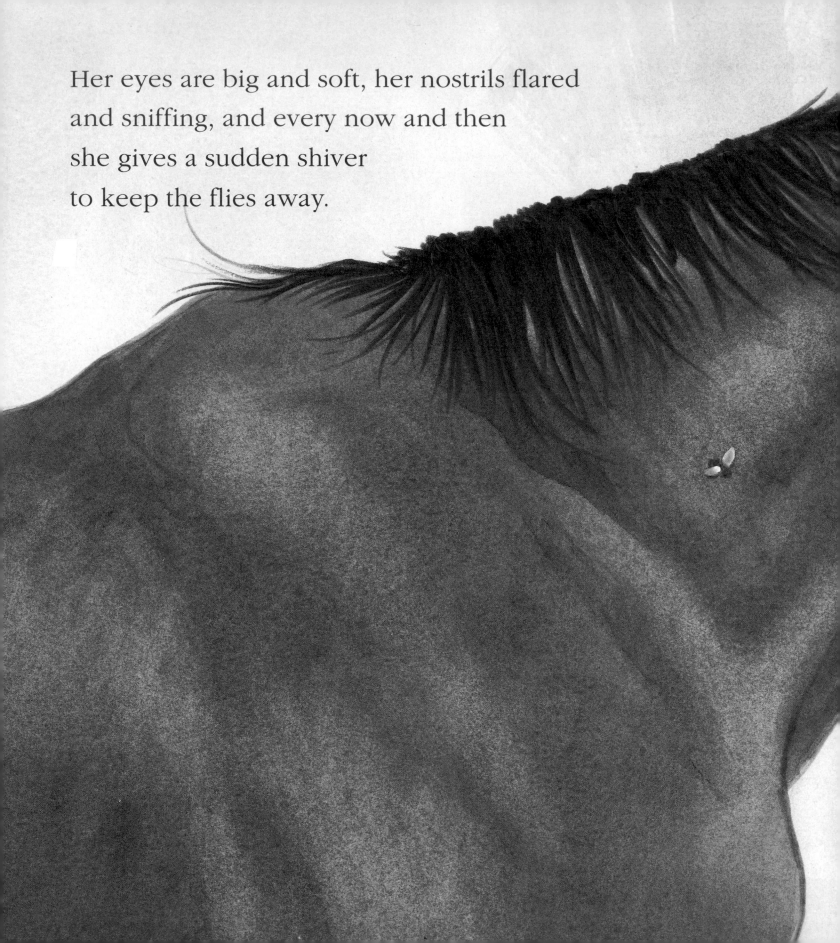

Watch her toss her mane
and arch her neck
and flick her ears
and blow down gently
through her nose.

Would you like to touch
her twitching nose?
It's silky soft,
but bristly too.

Would you like to make
the sounds she makes?
Horses whinny, horses snuffle,
horses nicker, snort, and neigh.

I love to smell her horsey smell.
It makes me think of muck and straw,
of earth and leaves and grass.

I love to watch her

walk

and trot

and canter

and gallop.

I love to watch her

buck

and rear.

I even love to watch her standing still.

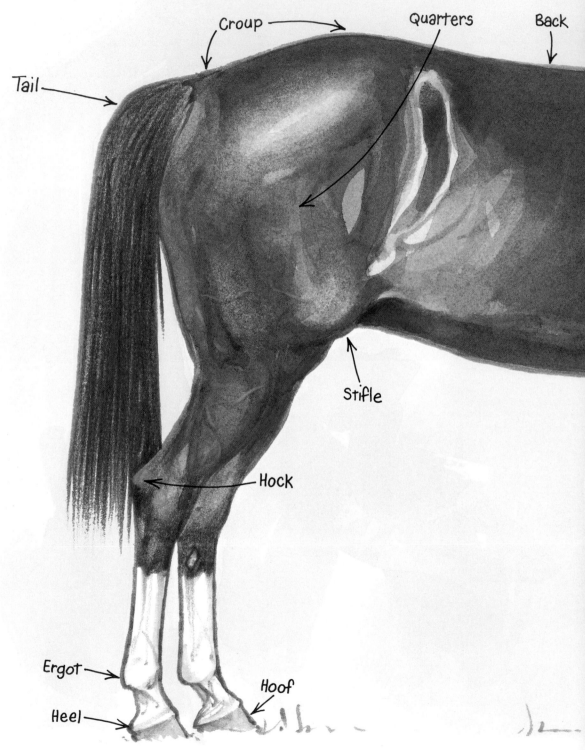

Croup

Quarters

Back

Tail

Stifle

Hock

Ergot

Hoof

Heel

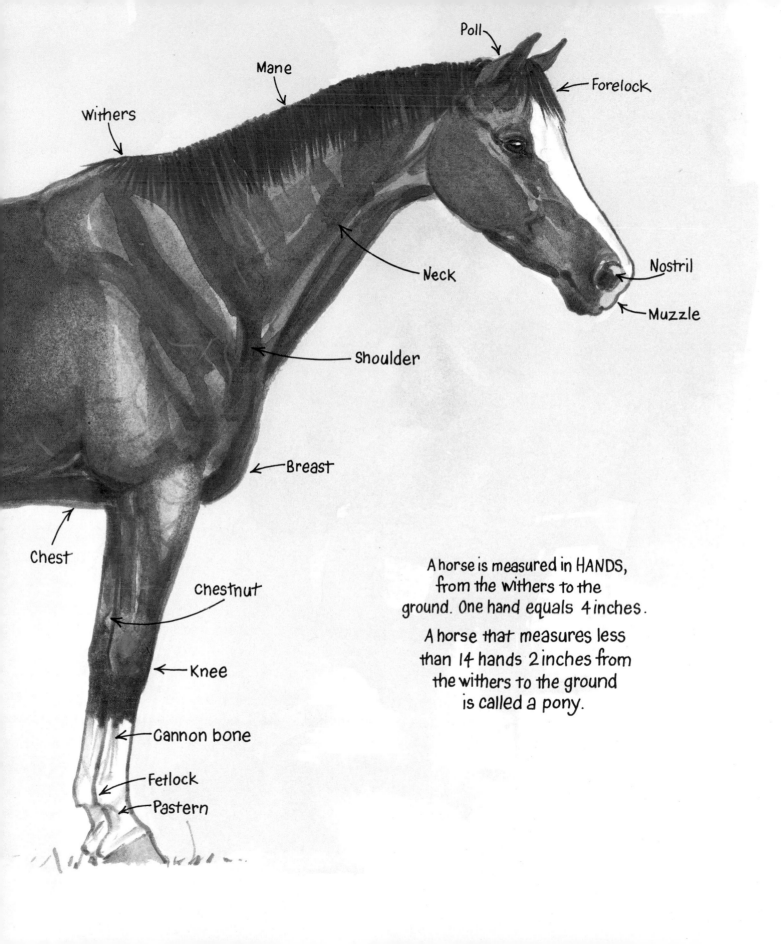

Poll

Mane

Forelock

Withers

Neck

Nostril

Muzzle

Shoulder

Breast

Chest

Chestnut

Knee

Cannon bone

Fetlock

Pastern

A horse is measured in HANDS, from the withers to the ground. One hand equals 4 inches.

A horse that measures less than 14 hands 2 inches from the withers to the ground is called a pony.

I love to watch her with her foal.

His head is small,

his body's short,

his legs are very long.

He jumps and kicks and starts to run.

And stops.

And dashes in a circle.

A newborn foal is wobbly on its feet
at first but quickly learns to walk.

If you could choose any horse,
which color would it be?

Piebald

Gray

Roan

Bay

Golden palomino

The skewbald or the golden palomino?
The black, brown, dun, or bay?
The chestnut, piebald, roan, or gray?

I have my favorite, but I love them all.
There's nothing I'd rather do
than just sit and be with horses.

There are
many horses
to look at
inside this
book—which
one is **your**
favorite?

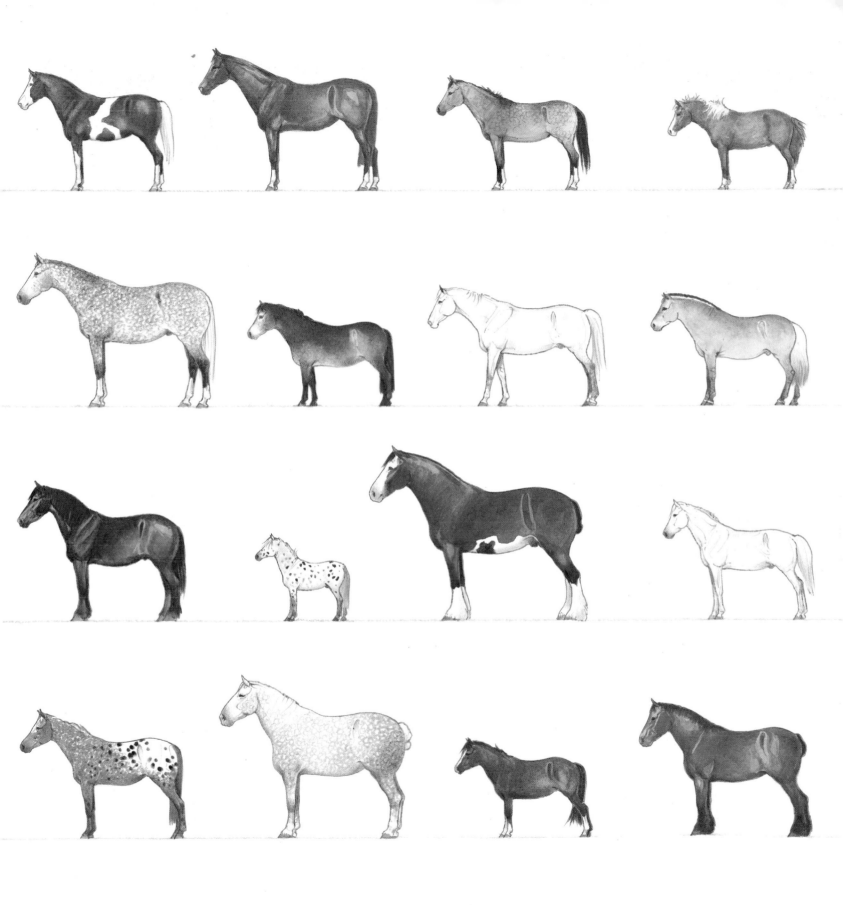

PETER HANSARD took children with him when he went to do research for this book. "We went to a nearby field," he explains, "and I watched to see what interested the children most. Then I created an 'ideal' paddock for the book filled with all shapes and sizes of horses so that I could show as much about them as possible." In addition to *A Field Full of Horses*, his works for children include *I Like Monkeys Because . . .* , and *Wag Wag Wag*, also in the Read and Wonder series.

KENNETH LILLY's grandfather was a farmer who trained horses, so he has been around them his entire life. In fact, it is family lore that, as an infant, he managed to crawl out of the garden and through a stable of twenty-one enormous farm horses, where he was later found seated in the last manger, next to a horse who was happily eating his oats. Also the illustrator of *Kenneth Lilly's Animals*, Kenneth Lilly is considered one of today's leading naturalist artists.